How to

The Ultimate Guide for Teens

Jennifer Love

Table Of Contents

Introduction

Chapter 1: Know How & Why You'll Want To Say "No"

Chapter 2: Peer Pressure in a Series of Steps

Chapter 3: Ways to Find Good Friends

Chapter 4: Getting Help

Chapter 5: Building Up the Courage To Say "No"

SPECIAL BONUS

Copyright 2014 by Globalized Healing, LLC - **All rights reserved.**

Introduction

Growing up as a teenager is not easy, and sometimes it can be depressing, lonely and sad – filled with people pressuring you to make choices that involve drugs, sex, violence, and even jail - but stay with me here because I am about to take you on a journey. Whether you are a pre-teen or an upper teen, you are going to be filled with knowledge and new ideas to prepare yourself for the realities of what being a teenager is *really* about.

Peer Pressure can make it hard to just say "no" when it seems like everyone is saying, "Don't worry, no one will find out. Everyone is doing it." It's hard and much easier to say you'll do it than actually do it!

The consequences of *not* saying "no" can include jail, destruction of relationships with friends and parents, and even death.

You will learn a proven-to-work, step-by-step process that includes strategies to resist all kinds of peer pressure. You'll learn the skills needed for dealing with all kinds of challenging situations that involve: ditching school, to drug use, to cheating and relationships issues, to lying to your parents, and much more!

Right about now, it's a good idea to perk your mind and ears up to what you are about to read in this book. Lets get started!

What Is Peer Pressure?

First of all, it is very important to understand what peer pressure really is. Peer pressure is pressure that you get from your friends, and other people your age. You know you are getting peer pressure when your friends are convincing you to do things that you do not really want to do. Often, what your friends want you to do is something bad, or even something that is against your beliefs and standards. Your friends do not even have to actually talk to you into doing something. If you have the slightest feeling to conform to the things they do, then that can be considered peer pressure.

It is during the teenage years when teenagers start to be classified as adults. With that king of classification, teenagers are vested very huge responsibilities not only at home, but at school as well. They are expected to do a lot of things just because 'they are not kids anymore.'

But at the same time, even if they are expected to act as adults, they are still treated as kids. Most teenagers still have bedtimes, TV times, and curfew. They still cannot hang out with the people they want, and they still are not given the liberty to make very important decisions. Having the responsibilities of an adult but the privileges of a child can definitely cause a huge toll on the psyche of a teenager.

Aside from that, teenagers also has to deal with hormonal changes. If you're a boy your voice will start to get deeper and you'll start developing body hair. You'll feel cravings that you've never felt before. All these changes make a teenager's life complicated. Thus, once negative peer pressure occurs, teenagers find themselves vulnerable and often too troubled to be focusing on resisting negative influences.

What causes peer pressure?

It can be quite tricky to pinpoint the exact causes of peer pressure. One has to study different social groups in order to come up with satisfactory findings. But one can always make assumptions on why teenagers influence other teenagers to do something they are not supposed to do.

Often times, it is the troubled teens who cause peer pressure. These are the teens who most likely have difficulties at home. Therefore, they have resorted to drug abuse, alcoholism, sex before they are ready, and other destructive habits.

Social groups usually develop a sense of camaraderie. They have this rationale of "we have to do all stuff, together." Thus, in a group of five friends, with four of them smoking and one is not, it would not be long before that non-smoker would start smoking. After all, he does not want to be different from the rest of the group.

Know How & Why You'll Want To Say "No"

Teen negative peer pressure can come in any form and in any shape. It is important that you know the different types of teen pressure so that you can deal with it properly.

Pressure to smoke and drink

Curiosity – this is one of the main reasons why teens succumb to teen pressure. Often, those who pressure their friends use curiosity as bait. "Wouldn't you want to know what this tastes like?" "You surely want to feel its effects, don't you?" Among most teens, and even pre-teens, there is always a curiosity to smoke and drink alcohol. As a child you might have pretended you were smoking a cigarette with some stick you found. You might even have pretended that the grape juice you were sipping was red wine or rum. Once your friends show you a pack of cigarettes, or even a bottle of beer, it can really be hard to resist your curiosity. Some teens really love the effect that cigarettes and alcohol gives them. Cigarettes give teens the feeling of a "high." It usually helps them calm down and forget about the troubles of life. For example, some teenagers find it especially necessary to smoke if they are troubled by an upcoming exam or anxious about asking someone out. Of course, there is also booze, which helps teens forget about the problems that they are facing. And it, should be noted, that drinking alcohol is a popular social past time among people. Liquor can help you loosen up and ease tensions. Thus, get-togethers are "more fun" whenever liquor is flowing. That is why there is always booze at parties.

It is usually during the pre-teen years when kids are first exposed to booze and cigarettes. There is usually that one classmate who somehow manages to steal cigarettes or beer and then brings them to school for his classmates to try. Of course, exposure to alcohol increases during high school. There will always be that one guy who uses a fake I.D. so he can purchase booze and cigarettes for high school parties.

Smoking and drinking are bad for your health. Let's start with smoking. There are a lot of sicknesses and conditions that are attributed to smoking.

- Stroke – Smoking can increase the chances of stroke. Stroke is one of the top causes of death not only in the United States, but in other parts of the world as well. If not fatal, a stroke can lead to temporary or permanent paralysis and severe brain damage. It should be noted that you can suffer from a stroke even if you are young.

- Lung cancer – Smoking can also cause lung cancer. In fact, it is the primary cause of lung cancer. Lung cancer is caused by the pollutants or carcinogens left in the lungs. Every cigarette stick contains at least sixty different types of carcinogens.

- Increased blood pressure – Another thing that smoking can cause is increased blood pressure. Smoking will damage your blood vessels by thickening them. Because they are thickened, the blood passageways grow narrower. When your blood pressure shoots up, the heart beats faster and can become damaged over time.

- Oral problems – Smoking can also cause a lot of oral problems. The most lethal problems include gum disease or even oral cancer. There are also other less-serious problems such as tooth decay, tooth and tongue discoloration, and even bad breath.

These are just the tip of the iceberg. There are so many other negative health effects of smoking aside from these. So we've heard about smoking, but what can alcohol abuse cause?

- Cardiovascular problems – Most of the cardiovascular problems that alcoholics experience have something to do with their alcohol abuse. If you get addicted to alcohol at a young age, there is a big chance you will suffer from cardiovascular problems if you do not change your habit. Some examples of such problems include cardiomyopathy, hypertension, and arterial fibrillation.

- Liver disease –The liver is a very important part of the body. It is the organ responsible for cleansing your blood. Without it, your blood would be filled with numerous intoxicants. A dirty liver can lead to the development of liver disease. Some of the indications of liver disease include vomiting of blood, extreme fatigue, and lack of appetite.

Pressure to do illegal drugs

Aside from being pressured to smoke and drink, you might also be pressured to do illegal drugs. Teens usually look at doing illegal drugs as something that cool kids do. Thus, if they do it, then they can be considered "cool" as well. There are numerous drugs out there that teens are usually pressured to take. First, there is marijuana. It is popular because a lot of people have easy access to it. Marijuana is a plant that can easily be grown at home. Also, it is something that kids can easily afford. Thus, it is very easy to find kids being pressured to "smoke a joint." Other drugs that are popular among teenage peers include ecstasy, heroin, cocaine, meth, and prescription drugs.

Most drug users were not really interested in doing drugs. Most of them are not even familiar with drugs. However, they happen to be with the wrong crowd. Their friends were the ones responsible for introducing drug use. Because of teen negative peer pressure, there are so many people these days who are addicted to drugs. Of course, drug overdose can result to death. Learn from those celebrities who overdosed on drugs.

Pressure to have sex

The teenage years can be a magical period in one's life. It is usually during this period where one starts to get attracted to the opposite sex in a serious way. And eventually, teens will find this one person whom they truly like. But of course, being officially in a relationship is not enough for most teens. Humans are just mere animals who have sexual desires. Thus, it is not a surprise that so many teenagers get pressured into having sex. "If you love me, then prove it." This is one of those sentences that can really convince a person to have sex even if he or she does not feel ready. Sometimes, teenagers get pressured to have sex not because of their own desires. Instead, they get pressured to do it because all their friends are doing it. And these days, being a virgin during the teenage years can make you a target for mockery.

Premarital sex is an issue that societies are facing today. It is an issue because some people who have engaged in it were just pressured or were even under the influence of alcohol. It is no surprise why there are a lot of young people who wake up in the morning regretting the things they did the night before. Not only do they suffer from shame and guilt, but they may also suffer from various types of sexually transmitted diseases. Of course, aside from those diseases, some even have unwanted pregnancies. Some of those who get pregnant unexpectedly choose to have an abortion, which in turn causes more guilt.

Pressure to skip class

School might seem like a bummer. If you feel like that while you are studying, that is normal. Every student can get lazy while studying. However, that does not mean that you have to ditch school. Education is important. As the saying goes, "knowledge is power." Things that are taught in school are things that can help you have a better life in the future. Unfortunately, peer pressure can cause anyone to skip classes. One does not simply skip class if no one wants to go with him. Usually, class skipping is done in groups. And if all your friends are skipping class and are planning to do something fun, it can be really difficult to say "no."

But what happens to those who skip class? There are so many teens out there who were not able to learn anything throughout the whole school year because they did not attend classes. They end up wasting so much of their precious time. What is alarming is that their parents are unaware of it. Those who skip class usually end up having to repeat another school year. In fact, those who skip class develop such a habit that some of them do not finish school.

Pressure to commit crime

Teen pressure is a very serious issue, especially since so many people get pressured to commit a crime. If you went to prisons, or even juvenile centers, you would most likely hear this – "My friends made me do it." You might say, "I would never commit a crime." But do not be so sure of that - especially if your peers are very good at convincing. Probably the most common crime related to peer pressure is stealing. So many teens have been forced to steal from their parents and other individuals close to them. If teens are not forced to steal from their parents, they are usually pressured to shoplift. It is alarming to find that peers can be influential and convincing enough to cause numerous individuals to break the law.

Peer pressure in a series of steps

Be careful - peer pressure can cause you to do a lot of things you do not like in a series of steps. For example, you are forced by your friends to drink. There is no harm in having a drink right? But you end up getting drunk. Since you are drunk and are out of your senses, one of your friends asks you to have sex with her. Even if you have not wanted to in the past, you suddenly agree upon a few jeers and cheers from your friends. Then, you end up impregnating the girl. Because you are depressed, your peers might offer you more booze and drugs to help you cope with your depression. You agree. Soon, you get addicted to drugs. But constant drug-use left you broke. Thus, you end up being convinced to steal from the old lady walking down the street. You see what happened in this example? What started out as a simple decision to drink beer with your friends ended up in a life that you did not dream of having. That is how big of an impact peer pressure can have on your life. What was stated above is just an example. Try your best not to get in a situation like this. Say "no" to peer pressure.

Three Ways Peer Pressure Can Change You

Almost every adult will warn, "Do not give into peer pressure because it can change you in a bad way." But how? Often, teenagers do not realize how peer pressure creates a negative impact on their lives. It is because of this that they easily give in to it. After all, "there is no harm in trying." However, peer pressure can definitely have a negative effect on your life if you succumb to it. Basically, it can change you in three steps – your interests will change, your beliefs will change, and your behavior will change.

Change of interests

Teen negative peer pressure can force you to be interested in things that you were not really interested in before. For example, there is alcohol. From a child, you were not really that interested in drinking it. But as you grew up and you became exposed to alcohol, with your friends pressuring you to do it, you ended up tasting it. Soon, whether you anticipate it or not, you will grow a liking for it. Regular alcohol consumption can lead to alcohol addiction and even abuse.

Most alcoholics would not drink any other beverage aside from alcohol. If the same thing happens to you, then you might start to forget the things that you were interested in before. Instead of your ordinary soda pops, you find yourself craving beer, vodka, rum, and any other alcoholic beverages. Again, there is the tendency to blend in with the crowd. Thus, you might end up changing your interests just so that they can jive with the interests of your peers. Another example would be regarding the aspect of skipping classes. School might once have been a fun place for you. But since your friends have no respect for the teacher and they start skipping classes, you might end up disliking school as well.

Change of beliefs

Next, there is the change of beliefs. Your beliefs change usually because you are trying to defend your change of interests. For instance, you did not like alcohol several years ago. But now that you are addicted to it, you might start making up excuses on why it is good. Thus, you might develop beliefs such as "it is okay to drink, I'm a grown up anyway," or "I don't care how alcohol can affect my health. What is important is that I'm enjoying it." Of course, a person's way of thinking is dramatically changed because of the things that he hears from his friends. "Schools are for losers!" or "Drugs make you cool" are just some twisted principles that one gets through peer pressure.

Morality starts to come into play. Past convictions are revolutionized. New life principles are developed. It is because of peer pressure that so many teenagers rebel against their parents. After all, the things that they have learned from their friends seem a lot better than the ones they have learned from their parents or any other authority.

Change of behavior

If one lets peer pressure change his beliefs, it would not be long before peer pressure affects his behavior as well. Again, the issue of conformity comes into play. A teenager has to conform in order to blend in. Of course, conformity requires actions. A person's actions can be affected by his interests and his beliefs. As mentioned earlier, interests and beliefs can change dramatically because of peer pressure. Thus, it is not a surprise that a lot of teens start to ditch school just to hang out with their friends. It is not a surprise that there are those who would rather lie to their parents than lie to their friends.

Probably the most affected aspect of behavior is the way one treats his parents. Often, peers promote themselves as the best people to be with, elevating themselves higher than parents. That is why so many kids and teens end up running away from their parents. They think that their parents are dumb. Aside from ruined relationships, peer pressure is also held responsible for so many youths that become pests to society. These are the youths who engage in vandalism and commit crimes. In short, peer pressure can definitely cause you to turn into a whole different person.

Ways To Find Good Friends

Hanging with the wrong people can definitely change your entire lifestyle. If you feel that you are getting negatively influenced by your friends, then it is probably time to look for new ones. Now, looking for friends can be a tough thing to do. This is especially true if you have bonded with your old friends for a very long time. However, things that bring you down definitely have to be let go. Here are some tips on how to look for new friends:

Look for positive influences

You want to have friends that can be positive influences on your life. For example, you might want to have a friend who is very interested in education and learning. A friend like that is a lot better than one who always wants you to ditch classes. You might also want to have a friend who has very high standards in life. Thus, you can expect a friend like that to encourage you to become a better person. You can even hang out with friends who can help you be busy at various other things such as playing computer games, playing sports, reading, and other acceptable norms. Meet new people! It will not hurt and it will definitely be good for you.

Look for friends in particular places

It has already been established that good friends are those who create positive impacts on your life. But these good friends can be a little bit tricky to find. Of course, the best tip for you to have a friend is to simply be one. If you become a friend to people you meet, you will not have a hard time expanding your circle of friends. You want to look for good friends in the right place. If you want smart friends, then you might want to hang out at the library. It is in there where you might meet a lot of people - ones who might be interested in the same bodies of knowledge that you are interested in. If you want friends who strive to live up to high standards in life, you might be interested to look for them in churches or youth recreational centers. Of course, there is no guarantee that you will not meet bad friends here. That is why you should still be on guard against peer pressure.

Be open to new interests

In order to increase your chances of meeting good friends, you might want to be open to new interests. For example, you might want to try your skills in playing basketball. You can go to the local basketball gym and meet new people there who can teach you how to play ball, or even some you can play basketball with. You can join an art class and meet other people interested in art. In school, you might want to start joining clubs. Expose yourself to new fields of interest. Through that, you will be able to find new passions as well as meet new, good friends.

Getting Help

Peer pressure is something that you do not have to fight alone. Battling peer pressure requires all the help that you can get. If you try to fight it on your own, you will end up succumbing to it. With the right support, anything is possible. There are so many people from whom you can get help.

Parents and Family

Friends may come and go, but there will always be your family. If you are dealing with peer pressure, it is always practical to get help from your parents. Share with them your struggles. You might be surprised at how helpful parents can be. Just look at the mother hen. She does everything for her chicks to grow up healthy and well. She always makes sure that they are safe under her wings. She always makes sure that they do not feel cold in the night. And she will attack those who will try to take her chicks from her. Your parents can be as protective as the mother hen. Do not be afraid to express to them your feelings. Tell them if you have some friends that are pressuring you. Not only can parents comfort you, but they might also be able to do something about those friends that are influencing you negatively.

Of course, there is no such thing as a perfect parent. If your parents are not there for you, you can always rely on other family members. You might have a caring brother or sister. Siblings can be your best pals. Yes, you might end up fighting or squabbling over a number of things. But in the end, they can still be a person you can rely on. After all, blood is still thicker than water. Family can definitely help you in your battle against peer pressure.

Good friends

As mentioned earlier, changing your friends might be practical, especially if they are influencing you negatively. However, you still might have some friends that are concerned for your well-being and would not pressure you to do bad things. Stick with those friends even more. If you do not have any good friends, start looking for some. They can definitely be a good support group. Isn't it nice to feel that you are not alone in your battle against peer pressure? Be with friends who can help you steer away from harmful vices. Be with friends who can influence you to be engaged in sports or do other things which will not do you any harm.

Counselors

Aside from family and friends, there are other people who can help you battle peer pressure. These are your counselors – people who can give very useful advice, as well as be your partners in battling peer pressure. For example, there is your school guidance counselor. Guidance counselors are very much acquainted with peer pressure, and they can easily help those individuals who are struggling with it. There are also spiritual advisers who are usually part of religious groups. They can give you spiritual advice and be part of your support group as well.

Of course, you can always consider getting help from professional psychologists or psychiatrists. Their input can be of great use, and they can also help you cope mentally with your current struggles. Getting help from counselors can definitely contribute in the development of your values, as well as your self-esteem. If you have fully developed values and a high level of self-worth, saying "no" to peer pressure can be very easy.

Chapter 6 – Building Up the Courage to Say "No"

'No.' It is a one-syllable word with two letters. As simple as the word is, it can be something that is very difficult to pronounce. This is because that word can have so many implications. Saying "no" can mean that you are refusing what could have been an enjoyable time with your friends. Saying "no" means that you are standing up for something. Saying "no" can even mean that you will look like a dork or a loser in the eyes of your friends.

The Psychology of Saying No

Why is it that people have a hard time saying "no"? Well, psychologists have given a number of answers. First of all, there is the feeling of not wanting to be rude. If your friends are drinking and they ask you to drink with them, would it not be rude to resist? Even if you do not want to drink beer, you take one out of simple courtesy. After all, you do not want to offend your friends. You do not want them to feel bad or even look bad.

Also, saying "no" can be especially hard when teen negative peer pressure seems to lead to new opportunities or experiences. You have not tried doing drugs before. But now that one of your friends is smoking a joint and he seems to be enjoying it, you suddenly start to become curious. Once he offers you the joint, you might have a hard time resisting. After all, you might not have the chance to be able to satisfy your curiosities in the future. The concept of closing doors to new opportunities or experiences is one of the reasons why people really have a hard time saying "no."

Of course, there is also that fear that something might happen to you if you say "no." So many individuals feel threatened by a lot of factors, and that is why they are forced to simply conform to peer pressure. For instance, a teen might feel that he will be rejected by his friends if he does not join them in a shoplifting stint. A teen might simply take drugs because he does not want to be in conflict with one of his friends. Fear can definitely have a grappling hold on an individual. Once fear gets hold of a person, his tongue can easily be tied, and he will definitely have a hard time saying "no."

Saying "No" Effectively

If your friends are asking you to do something bad or something that is against your morals, you can always say "no" proudly and with conviction. Doing so can help encourage you that you made the right decision. But of course, you might still consider those people as friends, even if they are influencing you negatively. Well, you can always say "no" in a calm and polite way.

Here is an example of a scenario wherein a teenager named Bill says "no" to his drug-addicted friends. "Come do drugs with us!" Bill's friends said. Bill, knowing how harmful drugs can be, decided not to do drugs with his friends, and said, "I'm sorry. But I have decided not to do drugs with you. I am afraid that it might ruin my health. It can ruin yours also. I promised myself that I would abstain from drugs. I hope that you respect my decision and I hope that you have the same decision as well." After saying that, Bill quickly walks away in order to avoid any further convincing and pressure that he might get from his "friends."

Saying "no" effectively requires you to say it like you mean "I don't want to" instead of "I can't." There is a big difference between the two. Say it with conviction and be proud of that decision. Do not leave a hint of hesitation. Once your friends get a trace of hesitation, they will definitely throw everything they have to make sure you conform to their wills. And when you say "no," try to leave as soon as possible. Do exactly as Bill did in the example above. Say it as soon as possible. Do not dilly-dally. If you do, you might end up getting convinced to give in to the demands of your peers.

Having the Courage to Say "No"

Having the courage to say "no" requires you to apply all the knowledge that you have obtained from this book. In chapter one, you were able to learn more about peer pressure and its causes. In chapter two, you were able to get acquainted to the different forms of peer pressure. As Sun Tzu, a famous military tactician, once said, "Know your enemy." If you know about the background of peer pressure, you will be able to deal with effectively. Also discussed in chapter two were the possible effects of peer pressure on your health. Of course, no one wants to suffer from diseases and other unfortunate consequences which resulted by giving in to peer pressure.

Chapter three discusses the steps on how peer pressure can totally change your lifestyle. Basically, you might end up being a totally different person if you succumb to it. Having a goal of preventing yourself from getting worse can definitely give you enough courage to say "no." Chapter four discusses the importance of choosing new friends. Sometimes, old friends can be so convincing that leaving them for new ones is a difficult, though practical solution. Of course, if you have a hard time dealing with peer pressure, you can always get help from certain people, which is discussed in chapter five.

Saying "no" does not seem so hard, does it? Go ahead and apply the things you have learned from this. Your life will be a lot better if you are strong enough to resist peer pressure.

We've come to the end already. Now you have the knowledge and skills to prepare yourself for all types of peer pressure. Use this to protect yourself and make the smartest decisions possible to continue advancing forward and making your future as awesome as possible!

Thank you and I wish you the best with your future!

Jennifer Love Books:

1.

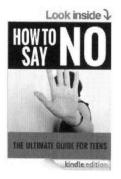

How To Say No - For Teens: The Ultimate Guide For Teens

2.

How To Make Friends - For Teens: The Ultimate Guide For Teens

3.

Fun Activities To Do With Your Kids: Includes 50 Fun Things To Do For Parents and Children

BONUS: Free Books & Special Offers

I want to thank you again for reading this book! I would like to give you access to a great service that will e-mail you notifications when we have FREE books available. You will have FREE access to some great titles before they get marked at the normal retail price that everyone else will pay. This is a no strings attached offer simply for being a great customer.

**Simply go to www.globalizedhealing.com to get free books.

Made in the USA
San Bernardino, CA
28 March 2019